Inspirations for Women
... a journey to wholeness

By Jacqueline Peart, Inspired by the Holy Spirit

Deep Calleth Unto Deep
Inspirations for Women...A Journey to Wholeness
Copyright © Jacqueline Peart

Cover design by Andy Colthart www.jharts.co.uk

Typeset by Get Set Go www.g-s-g.co.uk

Printed in United Kingdom by
Athenaeum Press Ltd, Tyne & Wear

International Standard Book Number: 0-9533060-3-8

This book or parts thereof may not be reproduced in any form without prior written permission of the publisher

Deep Publishing
PO Box 23606
London, E7 9TS
England

Scriptures marked (TLB) are taken from
THE LIVING BIBLE © 1971. Used by permission of
Kingsway Publications, Lottbridge Drove, Eastbourne,
East Sussex, BN23 6NT.

Scriptures marked (NKJV) are taken from the NEW KING JAMES VERSION © 1982 of the Holy bible by Thomas Nelson, Inc. All rights reserved.

Scriptures marked (TM) are taken from THE MESSAGE. Copyright © Eugene H. Peterson, 1993, 1994, 1995. Used by permission of NavPress Publishing Group.

Scriptures marked (AMP) are taken from THE AMPLIFIED BIBLE, Old Testament copyright ©1965, 1987 by the Zondervan Corporation. The Amplified New Testament copyright © 1958, 1987 by The Lockman Foundation. Used by Permission.

Scriptures marked (NIV) are taken from THE HOLY BIBLE NEW INTERNATIONAL VERSION®. Copyright ©1973, 1978, 1984 by International Bible Society. Used by permission of Zondervan Publishing House. All rights reserved.

Contents

Title	Page Number
Introduction	7
Section 1 – Getting Real… Let the Healing Begin	**17**
You've Grieved Long Enough!	22
Repent, Pursue Peace and Be Healed	25
Broken Hearts equal New Starts	28
You've Been Broken So That You Can Be Blessed!	31
Section 2 – Behind the Mask	**33**
God Longs for the Real You	37
Looking for Me	39
Behind Your Smile	41
Image	43
Alone Again	46
Section 3 – Leaving It Behind and Taking Off!	**49**
Wanted	54
Who Am I?	57
Your Future – A New Dimension	62
Woman – Your Change is Gonna Come!	65
Sisters Arise	69
Keep On Going	73
Section 4 – Celebrating My Past	**75**
My Father	80
My Mother	82
In Celebration of Our Elders	85

Section 5 – On My Way to a Better Future   **89**
Me   93
Single Mothers   95
Stronger Each Day   99
Who Can Find a Virtuous Woman?   101
Queens and Princesses   105

Section 6 – From the Father's Heart   **107**
I Am Searching   111
Dare to Dream…   114
Rise Daughter of Influence   119

Section 7 – Let the Journey Continue   **121**
Wholeness equal More of God!   126
Woman of Influence   127
Prayer of Commitment   129

Inspirations for Women
... a journey to wholeness

Welcome to the **Deep Calleth Unto Deep** series of books that have been developed to encourage, challenge and inspire you on your journey to wholeness in, with and through Jesus Christ!

Firstly, I would like to answer the question, 'Why *another* book for women with so many already on the market?' Because there are still so many of us living below spiritual fulfillment. My desire is to see women walk in their complete wholeness in Christ Jesus. My desire is to see us become enveloped in all the blessings the Father has for us, that we would judge ourselves against His standards and not the world's.

You see, the world will tell us that we must be a certain shape, shade, size and temperament. As we look at the popular magazines and adverts we can see how they try to depict images for us to aspire to. Many of us have fallen into the trap of trying to become that 'perfect' woman because of these social influences. If it's not the latest diet, it's the new face creams and fashion trends. We've even tried to become the perfect partner, parent, friend, employee, sibling and other roles that are part of our lives.

The media and the enemy have done a good job at trying to hold us in bondage desiring the fairy tale life. Unfortunately, or fortunately, there are no fairy tales in real life – that's for the films. We have a real life, and that makes our Maker even more real. You see, when we desire a fairy tale that is not achievable we start to fall short of one of the very tall orders placed on us by society (or we place on ourselves) and thus count ourselves as lacking or at worst failures. Only Superwoman, the fictional character, can achieve the type of perfection the world requires. But I believe God is not looking for superwomen, but real women, women who know who they are. Women who know their limitations, their strengths and their weaknesses, women who judge themselves to and by His word, not the world!

I mentioned in my first book in the series, *In Search of Wholeness*, that low self-esteem was something that followed me throughout my childhood and lest I had found the Lord it was preparing to hold me captive in my adulthood. I always felt less than other people. Somehow I didn't fit in with the 'popular' girls or 'cliques'. I always seemed to just miss the 'in crowd'. I wasn't pretty enough, trendy enough, slim enough, smart enough or, in some cases, bad enough, so at an early age, unbeknown to my own self at the time, I began my quest to fit in by wearing an acceptable mask.

The Webster's New World dictionary defines a mask as, '*anything that conceals or disguises and/or a protective covering for the face*'. So when I refer to a mask, I'm referring to anything that conceals or disguises your true identity (which is in Christ Jesus), anything that we have developed to protect ourselves from getting hurt. One of my masks was one of the *performer or entertainer*. I could always find something funny to say even if it was at my own expense, but somehow that didn't matter so long as I was accepted, so long as I was wanted. So long as was able to I fit in. What a high price to pay for acceptance, the loss of your identity!

I've seen where pain and disappointment have caused so many women to 'cop out of life', where they too have thought it easier to find an acceptable and in some cases an unacceptable mask to cover their pain and/or lack of esteem and knowing who they are. I believe that at a poignant point in our lives, albeit in childhood or adulthood, we knowingly or in the majority of cases unknowingly develop masks to make us appear acceptable to the wider world, our inner worlds and even to our families. So many women try to disguise their disappointment, shame, fear, guilt, uncertainty, childhood wounds, rejection, low self-esteem and doubts about themselves and where they fit in. Some try to hide through their jobs, through their partners, through their children or through their church as they strive for external success to hide their internal turmoil.

Since I began my journey with the Lord in 1995 my eyes have been opened to so much more. I can truly say I was naïve to much. If I met someone who was angry before, that person was just angry, or if I met someone who was promiscuous, that person was just plain promiscuous. Through my new eyes or should I say through my open eyes I now see more than people's quirks and idiosyncrasies. I now see their pain and longing. I see that anger when misplaced is not directed at me or their target but often at someone from their past and at worst aimed at themselves as frustration and sadness finds no other way to vent it self. So it is easier to shut everyone out rather than let anyone in and be hurt or disappointed again.

I now see promiscuity as a cry for help, a cry for intimacy and engagement, not just a moment of lust or physical pleasure but a cry for someone's acceptance and love.

I now see the businesswoman who is striving to be at the top of her business no matter the cost, becoming more ruthless than her male counterparts as a woman trying to prove something to someone. Whether that someone is herself, her siblings or more often than not one or both of her parents. There is an internal need for her not just to be successful privately but successful publicly as well. The need for affirmation is great as her desire is for that mother, that father, that sibling or grandparent to be proud of her. Why do I say all of this? How do I know this? I'm describing where I was before Christ Jesus intervened.

Reader, I worked my way up the corporate ladder to prove that I was good enough, that although I didn't get the qualifications I could have in school, I was someone and I could make it. I was striving for acceptance and approval from anyone and everyone including myself. Before I continue, I'm not saying that just because a woman is a career woman and is doing well she is hiding, running away from or trying to prove something. No, what I am saying is that when she is driven and her motives are about wanting to prove how successful she is, we need to realign our thinking about the reasons behind this. No job, no career or business can substitute love, acceptance and a real and right relationship with Christ.

Sometimes I'll sit and observe other women and an overwhelming feeling of compassion will come over me as I see how our lives can be distorted from what God's original intention was for us. You see, I'll observe the woman who has chosen to carefully dress herself so as not to attract too much male attention while she busily works around the church, home and job. She is almost obsessed with work as she pays penance for the abuse she suffered that was not her fault. She believes that by becoming

more spiritual or doing more good for God or society her efforts will somehow cleanse her from the shame and guilt that secretly plagues her. Yet, by accepting God all penance was and is paid, no need to work for it, no way we can earn it – Jesus loves you just as you are!
(John 15:13-15 NKJV)

I see the woman who always seems to be in love as she is torn by the feelings she has for the many beaus that pursue her, wanting the love and affection that she didn't receive from her emotionally or physically absent father. So a rumble under the sheets becomes a distorted way of feeling the strength and love of a man.

I see the woman who is desperately trying to keep her marriage together but the issues of her past have not been dealt with so she is unable to give of herself honestly, only what she thinks is expected of her. Why? Because she didn't know herself so how then could anyone else get to know her? Jesus is still the answer, the Word of God still the cure for unhealthy or unbalanced self-images and esteems. (Psalms 139)

I see the divorcee who desires to move on but is bound by guilt, bound by indecision and fear – 'What if I', 'Supposing I', so her life continues to move on outwardly but internally she is at stalemate. Even when she has chosen to marry again, her life moves on, another child, a new home but internally she still fights feelings of insecurity and fear that the past will repeat itself and so she over compensates by doing everything for her partner, not wanting to rock the boat. However, resentment secretly builds as she hopes for someone to release her from her prison of unmet needs. Christ has the keys to every prison and the good news is He came to set the captives free! (Luke 4:18 NKJV).

I see the single woman who is in her mid to late forties still believing God for her mate, getting on with life and achieving great things for the kingdom of God, businesses, real estate, yet secretly she wonders, 'Will it ever happen', 'What have I done to deserve this', 'Supposing I never…', 'What if I…' On occasions she may even seem bitter, but she is not; she is full of love and hope but every so often, fear and doubt manifests as anger. He is your beloved; you are cherished by Him and He is forever rejoicing over you, continue to hope in Him! (Songs of Solomon 2:16 NKJV)

I see the woman that is married and has all she ever desired: a husband, children and a wonderful home but although on the surface she is happy with her lot, she yearns deep within for more. She has spent so much time ensuring that everything was perfectly done that she forgot about looking after and understanding her own needs. Does that mean her family is not enough? No, it just means that there is more for her to know and to be. So on occasions when she hears of others doing great feats her response is tinged with a little resentment or even envy though she is pleased for others, and she still wonders what of her life – she desires more. All you need to do is ask God the Creator of everything to show you the fullness of your destiny, your purpose and mission. (Jeremiah 33:3 NKJV)

I see the mother who has weaned and nurtured her children. She has prayed for the day that they were old enough to take care of themselves. Yet when they are grown and she has no more need to worry, she still cannot help it. The weight of their future still lingers on in the back of and sometimes the forefront of her mind – still not yet free to be who she was created to be. Let God do it. Cast your burdens unto Him for He cares! (1 Peter 5:7 NKJV)

I see the grandmother old in age, grey in hair yet sharp as a pin. Wishing she could do more, wanting to move a little quicker, tired of being ignored. 'I understand', she says in her heart. 'I'm not gone yet', as the conversations go to and fro in front of her and around her. 'There's more', she says in her heart, 'God is not through with me yet. I still have ideas, ambitions and strength, though I suffer with a little high blood pressure and my bones aren't as strong, there is still more for me to achieve in the kingdom of God, if only my children would not worry so.' And she's right, there is more… (Psalms 92:12 – 15 NKJV)

I see the single mother that has had to do the job of two people yet at her best she is so thankful for the gift(s) she has been given as her children. She is so filled with joy and deep appreciation as she watches them grow and develop. Yet at her not so great times, the weariness begins to show, she's not as patient with little Suzie or Tommy. She is frustrated she cannot be there as much as she would like and twinges of guilt, regret and anger tries to taunt her over the separation of the children's father. God is a great Father, Dad and Husband – all we need to do is allow Him to be who we say that He is. (Isaiah 54:5, Psalm 68:5 & Matthew 16:13-17 NKJV))

I see the misunderstood teenager struggling for acceptance, fighting to find a place in a world system that rejects uniqueness and embraces likeness. She is miserable as puberty takes its toll, not quite a woman yet no longer a child. Who will understand her? Her parents seem to nag or want to solve all her problems, her friends are much in the same position but at least give a little comfort as they seek to find their own identity and way.

A word to teenage girls!

Young woman, your parents are trying to support you, not trying to control you or run your life for you. Sometimes they just cross the line in their desire to protect, support and nurture you. I know that you may feel as though your mother does not understand you and she may not. Why not teach her how to help you? Why not educate her in your language of need so you do not have to face your transition alone? She is not your enemy! There are some decisions she will make that will totally infuriate you but before you loose your cool, ask yourself these questions:

What was her motive? Did she do it to help me or harm me? Would she hurt me on purpose? What have I done to help her to understand my situation? Did I give her all the facts or lots of half-truths? If I lose my cool, what will it accomplish? Will it solve the problem or will the problem or issue still remain?

Sometimes it's easier to take out our frustration on our loved ones. Young woman, decide today to celebrate your relationship with your mother and instead of pulling or fighting against her, learn to work with her, faults and all, because that is what she has committed to do with you. Why? Because she loves you more than you could ever comprehend.

There is so much more that I see as I go through life and I'm sure at some point you'll hear more about it in another one of my books or conferences. What I wanted to do by sharing some of my thoughts and observations with you is to enable you to reflect on how you see others, but not just how you see them but how you see you! The next time you see someone that is behaving promiscuously, or says they are pleased for you when something happens, yet you sense there is something amiss, remember we are all still a work in progress. As you travel along your own journey to wholeness with God you can share this book and your testimony with the women you meet. Share how you recognised that manmade masks or shields are not the answer but finding out who you are in Christ was and is!

A good starting place in your journey to wholeness would be to grab a pen and a piece of paper and answer the following questions:

- What is your earliest memory of not fitting in with a group or individual?
- How did you feel about not fitting in? Describe your feelings at the time.
- Did you tell anyone about how you felt or did you keep it hidden?
- What did you do to manage the disappointment of not fitting in?
- Do you think you wear a mask? If so, what would it look like?
- Why do you wear a mask?
- What do you need to do to come out from behind the mask?
- What do you need to do to work on your own God self-esteem?
- What do you need to do to work on your relationship with God?
- What do you need to do to become all that God has created you to become?

For some of you reading this, you may be struggling with the idea of masks and may even be feeling irritated by the mere suggestion that you might be wearing one.

Let me share some of my story…

I am the youngest of three sisters whom I love immensely. At an early age I decided that they, in my opinion, were much smarter than I. This was borne out in school when teachers would make comments about my ability in certain areas. For example, Marcia is an amazing illustrator and so all my art teachers expected me to be good at art. I wasn't! Similarly, Yvonne, my eldest sister, was great at law and history, so my teachers would comment on my ability or lack of it. These comments fed messages to me that I was not as good as my siblings and, more deeply than that, I received these messages as confirmation. So, as mentioned before, subconsciously I began to play the role of the 'performer' and 'entertainer' to be liked and to be accepted through another route because I realised that academically I was not going to make my mark. Throughout my career and life, up until the time I met Christ Jesus – or should I say *He met with me*, I was oblivious to the fact that I covered my disappointment, sadness and lack of acceptance by trying to be liked. I hungered for approval.

In 1997 I prayed a simple prayer: 'Lord, make me whole, make me be all you created me to be.' At that point my journey started. God began to show me how I compromised myself because of my need to be liked, loved and accepted. He began chiseling away at my character and personality, showing me my manmade strategies and showing me through His word, His strategies. Psalm 139 was crucial to my deliverance and journey, understanding that He made me, He knitted me together in my mother's womb, He watched me being formed and that even when I was at my lowest point, He was there still with me. That was an awesome revelation for someone who was playing catch up!

I'm still allowing God to chip away at all the manmade and self-made masks and self-protection mechanisms that I have developed and it is truly a beautiful, yet at times uncomfortable and painful, process. Is it worth it? Yes, every bit! When I see the Father in me and in my actions there is a joy and peace that words cannot explain. When I see His image in me (Genesis 1:27) and I realise my beauty (Psalms 139:14), my power (Luke 10:19-20), my authority (Genesis 1:18 & Mark 11:23), my peace, gentleness, love, goodness, kindness, faithfulness, long-suffering and self control (Galatians 5:22,23), all I can do is give Him all the Glory and praise and wonder why I fought to stay where I was with behaviours that were unhealthy and crippling to my development.

I hope sharing my firsthand experience has helped some of you reading this think more deeply about how and why masks develop.

I'd like to share a special note for Christians. Being a Christian does not equal being perfect even though we are being perfected in Jesus day-by-day. Being perfected is very different to being a perfectionist. When you are being perfected you allow God to do the work, when you are being a perfectionist you are doing the work! I believe one of the biggest gifts we can give back to God is true worship (John 4:24). There is something about worship that when you reach into the 'Holies of Holies' you have to be real. You have to put aside all the facades, all the religious rhetoric and become naked, but not ashamed, before the Lord. I don't believe God is looking for superwomen to come into His Sanctuary, women who know all the right words to sing, long prayers to pray. I believe He is looking for women that are prepared to be broken to become whole. Those who desire truth in their inward parts (Psalms 51:6), those who are willing to come as they are, willing to come with a broken and contrite heart (Psalms 51:17).

I want to be real! I want to be whole! How about you?

The Webster's New World dictionary defines 'real' as 'authentic, genuine, not pretend, sincere'. I want to be authentic, the 'Real Deal', just what God intended and made me to be. God help me; help us to be genuine, not pretend but sincere!

My desires through this ministry and through these books are to see God's children come into the full knowledge of who God is and who we are in Him, that we would know His will for our lives, wholeness and prosperity, whether emotional, physical or spiritual.

I am fully persuaded that God has so much more for each one of His daughters. God loves each one of us with an everlasting love and He is not moved by our past no matter how bad or sad it was. He will love you and treat you like the royalty you are and deserve if we will only allow Him to (1 Peter 2:9 NKJV).

I pray that as you read this book of inspired poetry and thoughts, the anointing that destroys yokes and removes burdens (Isaiah 10:27) will come upon you, and you will dig deeper into Him to find out more about you *...for deep truly does call unto deep* (Psalm 42:7 NKJV).

Be blessed and encouraged

Let the journey begin…

Section 1: getting real... let the healing begin

Pg 1139

Do not be conformed to this world (this age) (fashioned after and adapted to its external, superficial customs), but be transformed (changed) by the (entire) renewal of your mind (by its new ideals and its new attitude), so that you may prove (for yourselves) what is the good and acceptable perfect will of God, even the thing that is good and acceptable and perfect (in His sight for you).

Romans 12:2 AMP

Romans 12 vs 1-2 (message)

So here's what I want you to do, God helping you. Take your everyday, ordinary life - your sleeping, eating, going to work, and walking around life - and place it before God as an offering. Embracing what God does for u is the best thing u can do for him.

Don't become so well-adjusted to your culture that u fit into it without even thinking. Instead fix your attention on God. You'll be changed from the inside out. Readily recognise what he wants from u. and quickly respond to it. Unlike the culture around you, always dragging u down to its level of immaturity, God brings the best out of u. develops well-formed maturity in u.

Section 1 – getting real… let the healing begin

getting real…let the healing begin

To begin your journey to wholeness you must first get real so God can begin the healing process in your life. Getting real will take some action on your part. That action may mean you have to make the decision to step out of your comfort zone, it may mean facing up to some of the masks you have been wearing or it may mean going to God and just asking Him to show you, you!

Whatever it is for you it will take some kind of a decision (Deuteronomy 30:19 –20 TM). It starts in your thinking first. You must make up in your mind to become all God has created you to be, so you can begin living in wholeness.

Pg 209 (handwritten)

I just want to prepare some of you reading this by saying, asking God to make you whole can result in you first becoming broken. This was my experience. It felt like from the minute I prayed – what I felt was a relatively simple prayer for the Lord to make me whole – I felt as if my life began to fall apart. All the things that I had built up, all my coping strategies and mechanisms stopped working and I had to go to God for everything. I had to give up control and instead of making sense of my life through my own eyes, God began to show me His divine plan for my life through His eyes!

Needless to say I went through a process of mourning because I had to let some 'good' as well as the bad stuff in my life die so what God had for me could live. This included asking God to forgive me for some of the choices I had made previously. I also had to forgive the people in my life that I believed were responsible for where I was, my parents included.

You see, we can hold individuals in our past accountable for where we are in our present. Can I just say that it is true that our parents moulded us and shaped us through their parenting skills but the reality of it is they too are growing, learning and developing. We cannot take people where we haven't been ourselves. For example, it is so interesting to see your parents become grandparents and watch how they make different choices for your children. What they would have gone crazy over when

Deep Calleth Unto Deep

you were a child, they now just smile and say 'Oh leave them, it doesn't matter' – a big change in some cases! They have done what we need to do and that is to learn from the mistakes they made and turn them into life lessons that change their current reality. In other words, we have to quit blaming them for everything and decide to forgive and move on.

Section 1 – getting real... let the healing begin

So let's get real and let the healing begin...
The Spirit of the Lord God is upon Me,
To preach good tidings to the poor;
He has sent Me to heal the brokenhearted,
To proclaim liberty to the captives,
And the opening of the prison to those who are bound;
To proclaim the acceptable year of the Lord,
And the day of vengeance of our God;
To comfort all who mourn,
To console those who mourn in Zion,
To give them beauty for ashes,
The oil of joy for mourning,
The garment of praise for the spirit of heaviness;
That they may be called trees of righteousness,

Isaiah 61: 1-3 NKJV

you've grieved long enough!

Daughter you've grieved long enough,
It's time to come forth out of your mourning, for joy awaits you,
It's time to take off your sackcloth and ashes and return to the joy of your salvation!

How long will you grieve for things long gone,
Your past mistakes,
Those broken relationships,
Those feelings of inferiority, that desire to fit into the clique,
How long will you grieve about your status, albeit marital, financial, social or spiritual?
How long will you mourn in your heart?
Cry out in your sleep as you endeavour to live a life pleasing to *others*?

Daughter you have grieved long enough!

Put your hand over your heart and speak to yourself as you repeat these words with Me...

I have grieved long enough
It's time to come out!
Today, I forgive myself for not being all that I had dreamed about being and all others expected me to be.
I forgive myself for setting myself false and unrealistic expectations,
Goals that only a superwoman could keep, like
Never sinning, never falling short of the grace of God, like not being a perfect parent/partner (whatever that is) or being the perfect size, complexion and build (whatever that is).
Today I choose to stop mourning; I choose to stop grieving as I hearken unto the word of the Lord.
I receive beauty for ashes,
I receive the oil of joy in exchange for mourning and
The garment of praise in exchange for the spirit of heaviness!

I arise today!

For I have grieved long enough and it's time to come out!

I arise today forgiven and accepted,
I arise today for I am needed and wanted,
Blessed and empowered,
Washed and cleansed by the blood of Jesus!

Today I arise for my days of grieving old things are over!

Hallelujah!

Today I will no longer have my Past in front of me.... but will put it behind me, where it belongs.
Tomorrow I will start a free walk with god –

'And you shall love the Lord your God with all your heart, with all your soul, with all your mind, and with all your strength.' This is the first commandment.

And the second, like it, is this; 'You shall love your neighbor as yourself.' There is no other commandment greater than these.

Mark 12:20-21 NKJV

And make straight paths for your feet, so that what is lame may not be dislocated, but rather be healed. Pursue peace with all people, and holiness, without which no one will see the Lord; looking carefully lest anyone fall short of the grace of God; lest any root of bitterness springing up cause trouble, and by this many become defiled.

Hebrews 12: 13-15 NKJV

'In prayer there is a connection between what God does above and what you do. You can't get forgiveness from God, for instance, without also forgiving others. If you refuse to do your part, you cut yourself off from God's part.

Matthew 6:14 TM

repent, pursue peace and be healed

God is a jealous God, who desires all of you,
Not just a part of you.
That includes your heart, mind, soul and body.
This is not an optional extra but it's the first commandment He gives to us!

The second commandment is to love your neighbour as yourself,
Yet so many of us have not yet learnt to love ourselves so how can we truly love our neighbours?

A good start in getting real is firstly to repent, that is confess the sins that you have committed against God and your fellow man.
Sisters, it's easier to say than sometimes to do,
So if there is a person who you know has hurt you and forgiving them does not feel like an option,
Then think about how you would feel if God did not, and or would not, forgive you a sin of your past!
Forgive them until it stops hurting,
Forgive them until peace springs up from your very belly,
Seventy times seven times if you must,
Because forgiveness releases a balm of joy and release that resentment, bitterness and anger cannot.

'You don't understand: she caused the break up of my marriage',
'I trusted them and they betrayed me',
'He left without a word',
'He never said they loved me',
'She always treated her better than me'.

Whatever the heartache, repent for holding it in. Forgive them so that you might be forgiven, for Sister, it's truly time to let the healing begin…
With real repentance and forgiveness taking place you are then in the position to pursue peace!

Inspirations for Women . . . A Journey to Wholeness

One of the definitions of peace is the 'absence of war',
Another definition is wholeness,
So if you truly desire to begin your journey to wholeness you must pursue peace.

How?

By pursuing first and foremost the God of peace, Jesus Christ, Jehovah Shalom,
Then rid yourself of all the issues in your life that cause you drama and frustration.
This may be certain social groups; it could be that male friend who after five years still cannot commit. It could be things in your diet that you know causes you to be down and weary, whatever it is,
It's time to get real.

Let them go!

For Sister it's time to let the healing begin…

Forget about what's happened;
Don't keep going over old history.
Be alert, be present, I'm about to do something brand-new.
It's bursting out! Don't you see it?

Isaiah 43: 18–19 TM

My sacrifice (the sacrifice acceptable) to God is a broken spirit;
A broken and contrite heart (broken down with sorrow for sin and
humbly and thoroughly penitent), such, O God, You will not despise.

Psalm 51: 17 AMP

You will show me the path of life; in Your presence is fullness of joy,
at Your right hand are pleasures for evermore

Psalm 16:11 AMP

broken hearts equal new starts

I can remember in the recesses of my mind the line of a song that goes something like 'What becomes of the broken hearted?'

Well I finally found the answer and it's not what it used to be. Before I became a real woman I'd adopt one of two strategies:

Strategy 1 – Act like it didn't bother me and carry on life as normal. Okay, so you eat more ice cream and potato chips; okay, so you smile falsely and snap at the least possible thing, but it seemed to work. Or did it?

Then there's:

Strategy number 2 – Wail, and wail, weep and holler, call your best friend and discuss it for hours – that always makes you feel better. And of course it is always the other person's fault or else how would we be superwomen if we were not suffering for (another) a good cause?

Then I found Jesus!!!

The awesome lover of my soul,
Then I found the broken heart mender,
My friend and my beau,
That's when I became a real woman...because there was a real man in my life!

I realised that every time my heart was broken it gave me the opportunity for another start.
That's when I found out that a *broken heart equals a new start!*

No point fussing, no point moaning, no point wondering 'if only' and 'why'. Get into the presence of God; get into the Master's face!

And get ready – it's time for a new start!

Section 1 – getting real… let the healing begin

So if your heart is broken today,
If you are wondering why and how you will go on,
Believe me; I'm not trying to be super spiritual or 'holier than thou',
Because my Sister I've been there too many times.
In fact I'm there right now!

But today I got into the Master's presence and I feel the healing in my bones,
I sensed His warmth after the first tear drop,
For Daddy God responds to tears, He responds to our cries.
So if it's a relationship that's gone wrong,
A friend who has betrayed you,
A church brother or sister has disrespected you as you hoped for better from them,
Get into the Master's presence and you'll realise that nothing else matters!

Remember:

A broken heart = a new start

What is God trying to start in your life?
What have you been praying for, hoping for?
What new start does He have for you?

For, in my experience, broken hearts always equal new starts!

Therefore if the Son makes you free, you shall be free indeed.

John 8:36 NKJV

The thief comes only in order to steal and kill and destroy. I came that they may have and enjoy life, and have it in abundance (to the full, till it overflows).

John 10:10 AMP

…Nor give place to the devil.

Ephesians 4:27 NKJV

But the fruit of the (Holy) Spirit (the work which his presence within accomplishes) is love, joy (gladness), peace, patience (an even temper, forbearance), kindness, goodness (benevolence), faithfulness, gentleness (meekness, humility), self-control (self-restraint, continence).

Galatians 5:22-23 AMP

you've been broken to be blessed!

You've been broken so that you can be blessed!
That's a strange comment to make
But that's just the way it is.

Struggles
Trials
Temptations
Frustrations
Irritations and even some Spiritual manifestations.

You're being broken so that you can be blessed!

We're only broken for a while and then blessings do come.
Sometimes our prayers are answered with brokenness,
Mmm, so what have you been praying for lately?
But it's just so that we can be whole and blessed.
Other times our suffering is prolonged
For we haven't truly let go and let God.
We haven't looked at where we are in the situation,
Looked at ourselves for the clue to making it easier;
The world isn't against us,
God certainly isn't either.
Your finances aren't against you,
Neither your work, church, family nor friends.

There is an enemy we war against.
His mission is to kill, steal and destroy!
Have you made a way for him to enter?
Have you made room for his wiles?
Have you been dismayed when you should have prayed?
Been self righteous when you should have sacrificed?
Been miserable when you could have been praising?

You know we're broken so that we can be blessed.
As God works on you,
As He develops the fruits of the Spirit in your life,

Inspirations for Women . . . A Journey to Wholeness

It's so that you can handle all your blessings!
The exceedingly abundantly and above all you can imagine blessings are the ones that I'm referring to.
The blessings that make you the head and not the tail,
Above and not beneath
The victor and not the victim, in this precious walk of ours!

So as you allow the Spirit of God to lead
Sometimes you'll be broken my friend!

If you are facing a trial,
A temptation, frustration or irritation,
If you feel you've waited long enough
And it's all that other persons fault,
If only they would listen,
If only you had the finances you could…
If they would only…
If I could just…

Maybe He desires to increase the fruits in your life…
Is it love,
Joy,
Peace,
Longsuffering,
Kindness,
Goodness,
Faithfulness,
Gentleness or self control?
Or maybe it's patience or humility?

You're being broken so that you can be blessed!
It may start out feeling hard and in some cases unfair,
But it's just for a while my Sister,
Because as you become more led by the Spirit,
As you put your flesh to death,
You'll understand what I'm trying to say:

You've been broken so that you can be blessed!

Jeremiah 29 vs 11 (Pg 789)

Section 2 behind the mask

But what happens when we live God's way? He brings gifts into our lives, much the same way that fruit appears in an orchard – things like affection for others, exuberance about life, serenity. We develop willingness to stick with things, a sense of compassion in the heart, and a conviction that a basic holiness permeates things and people. We find ourselves involved in loyal commitments, not needing to force our way in life, able to marshal and direct our energies wisely.

Legalism is helpless in bringing this about: it only gets in the way. Among those who belong to Christ, everything connected with getting our own way and mindlessly responding to what everyone else calls necessities is killed off for good – crucified.

Since this is the kind of life we have chosen, the life of the Spirit, let us make sure that we do not just hold it as an idea in our heads or a sentiment in our hearts, but work out its implications in every detail of our lives. That means we will not compare ourselves with each other as if one of us were better and another worse. We have far more interesting things to do with our lives. Each one of us is an original.

Galatians 5:22-26 TM

behind the mask

Within the introduction I expounded on the idea of wearing masks. Whether consciously or not, the reality is that we often think we need to be someone other than the person that God created us to be. The author of *The Message* captures this sentiment beautifully in his translation of Galatians 5: 22-26 where he captures the Father's heart about how we ought to live.

When we are judging ourselves by each other and not by our Creator, one of us will think we are either better or worse off than the other. But when we live according to God's rule and word, we become more and more like Him; no need to wear a mask, just being true to who we are and to whom we came from.

Sharing a real example of this comes from my first few years of becoming a Christian. I used to listen to other people pray and I always felt that I wasn't quite good enough because I couldn't remember scriptures as well, or because I stopped praying before the more mature saints ceased. There were times when I would start to repeat what I had already prayed just so I would not look as though I hadn't missed it and I too was just as holy.

God had to take me from behind that religious mask and teach me about real and right relationship with Him. Through books, conversations and His word, He began to reveal to me how differently He dealt with all of His children, not one the same. Not one fingerprint or DNA the same as another, that each person has a different call and gifting upon their life. What a relief! We don't' have to pray, laugh, dance, speak or be anything like any one other than ourselves.

Every so often when I feel uncertain about a situation and I compare myself, or try to match up with another I am reminded that I'm out of alignment with who God says I am. In effect I put back on my mask. I have to remind myself that I am unique, not the same, but as special, bought with a price, fearfully and wonderfully made, and that as long as I try to fit in, I wear a mask and deny and rob this world of the unique gift and style God has placed within me.

God reminds me that I don't' have to use a mask to protect myself because He has and will always be my Protector!

Behind the mask…

Then God said, 'Let us make man in Our image, according to Our likeness; let them have dominion over the fish of the sea, over the birds of the air, and over the cattle, over all the earth and over every creeping thing that creeps on the earth.'

So God created man in His own image; in the image of God He created him; male and female He created them.

Genesis 1:26-27 NKJV

Yet amid all these things we are more than conquerors and gain a surpassing victory through Him Who loved us.

Romans 8:37 AMP

god longs for the real you!

God longs for the real YOU!

Who are you?
Where do you come from?
Where are you going?
Why are you here?
What's your purpose in life?

Until you can answer all of the above
A facade we create,
A mask for us to survive,
A place for us to hide,
Or is it self-protection we call it?

God longs for the real YOU!

You're prettier than you think,
You're more intelligent than you know
And no degree or qualification can determine the wisdom I give to you.

You're more able than you believe,
You see, you're more than a conqueror,
You are an over comer,
Stronger than anything you care to put a name to.

God longs for the real YOU!

Stop looking at the world for approval and acceptance;
Take a peep from behind your mask.

Then you'll realise that
God is the beginning and the end of the real you!

Deep Calleth Unto Deep

Oh Lord, You have searched me and known me.
You know my sitting down and my rising up;
You understand my thought afar off.
You comprehend my path and my lying down,
And are acquainted with all my ways.
For there is not a word on my tongue,
But behold, Oh Lord, You know it altogether.
Such knowledge is too wonderful for me.

Psalms 139: 1 - 4, 6 NKJV

And you will seek Me and find Me, when you search for Me with all your heart.

Jeremiah 29:13 NKJV

Section 2 – behind the mask

looking for me!

Anyone found me?

I'm looking for me!

I'm a little girl masquerading as a woman.
I got lost along the way, wanting to be all for everyone,
I didn't leave anything for me.

Anyone found me?
I'm looking for me, the real me!

I'm a mother, a sister, a lover, a friend, my different roles I play well.
An Oscar winner I could be.

But has anyone found me?
I'm looking for me!

I'm professional, I'm witty, charming as well,
But has anyone seen me?
I'm looking for me!

Like a pressure cooker I'll explode if I don't find me soon.
Has anyone found me? I'm looking for me...

Ssh my child,

Before you were born, I named you and ordained you.
Rest with Me a while, for my yoke is easy and my burden is light.

You're who I say you are.
When you search for Me with your whole heart you'll find the Me
you're looking for.

Deep Calleth Unto Deep

'Before I shaped you in the womb,
I knew all about you.
Before you saw the light of day,
I had holy plans for you:
A prophet to the nations –
That's what I had in mind for you.'

Jeremiah 1:5 TM

There is no fear in love; but perfect love casts out fear, because fear involves torment. But he who fears has not been made perfect in love. We love Him because He first loved us.

1 John 4:18-19

behind your smile

What hides behind your smile?
Your smart clothes and your fine hairdo?

What hides behind your smile?
Pain of the past,
No understanding of your present so you become anxious about your future!

You're beautiful
So don't hide behind your smile
Praising, praying, singing, worshipping, jumping and dancing,
But I see behind your hallelujahs and behind your praise the Lords.

If you could see what I see,
If you knew what I knew,
If you could hear what I hear,
You'd know that no one can harm you.
For the Lord says, 'I have chosen you, ordained you.
I know you've been waiting to get found out,
Waiting for something to go wrong;
You can exhale,
Yes you can breathe again.
Daughter you don't have to hide behind your smile.
You see, when I died I liberated you,
Through my death I gave you life.
Live it, live it in truth,
Live it like it was your last!'

Take a peep,
Step out,
You'll see what I have been waiting for;
A life of liberation,
A life of real smiles, real laughter and joy that can only be found in the Father!

For now we are looking in a mirror that gives only a dim (blurred) reflection (of reality as in a riddle or enigma), but then (when perfection comes) we shall see in reality and face to face! Now I know in part (imperfectly), but then I shall know and understand fully and clearly even in the same manner I have been fully and clearly known and understood (by God).

1 Corinthians 13: 12 AMP

For I know the thoughts that I think toward you, says the Lord, thoughts of peace and not of evil, to give you a future and a hope.

Jeremiah 29:11 NKJV

And He said to me, 'My grace is sufficient for you, for My strength is made perfect in weakness.'

2 Corinthians 12:9 NKJV

image

When you look into the mirror,
What image do you see?

Who is it that stares back at you?
What image do you see?
A woman or a little girl?
Your mother or your father?
Your present, your past or your future?

When you look into the mirror,
What image do you see?
A friend, or an enemy, the real you or a façade of the real you,
someone everyone else wants you to be?

When you look into the mirror,
What image do you see?
An image of strength or an image of weaknesses?
An image of failure or success?
Fear or hope?
Wasted life or opportunities?

When you look into the mirror,
What image do you see?

If it's negative, it's time to clean your mirror with a spray of positivism!
For the mirror in which you need to look is called the Word of God!
This mirror does not discriminate against your figure, shade or dress.
But it defines your beauty, your attitude, your ability and destiny.
You see, you're created in His image,
Fearfully and wonderfully made.

He knows the thoughts He has towards you,
Thoughts of peace and not evil, that give you a future as well.
In your weakness His strength is perfect,
In your not enough He is more than enough.

When you look into the mirror,
What image do you see?

Now take another look in that mirror and make a decision about what you will see.

A clearer picture should now be reflected from the solid, unfailing word of God.

So every time you look in the mirror remember the words of this poem,
You are not defined by the world's standards,
You're an exact replica of the King!

Written on the 4th September 1999 while with Donna, Ronica and Yvonne USA

...and be satisfied with your present (circumstances and with what you have); for He (God) Himself has said, I will not in anyway fail you *nor* give you up *nor* leave you without support. (I will) not, (I will) not, (I will) not in any degree leave you helpless *nor* forsake *nor* let (you) down (Relax My hold on you)! (Assuredly not).

Hebrews 13:5 AMP

alone again

What shall I do now?
Read a book,
Play a computer game,
Go for a walk,
Mmh, I know, I'll call a friend.

Ring, ring, ring, click as the answer machine goes on...
Hi, sorry we're not available to take your call right now, but if you'd like to leave a message after the tone we'll get right back to you as soon as we can...

I know, I'll call another friend.

Ring, ring, ring, click as the answer machine goes on...
Hi, sorry we're not available to take your call right now, but if you'd like to leave a message after the tone we'll get right back to you as soon as we can.....

I'll try one more friend.

Hi, how you doing?
I'm well; we were just about to take the kids to the park. I'll give you a call tomorrow.

Alone again. I ponder as the phone begins to ring...

Another friend calls to go to a social gathering,
I jump at the opportunity yet even in the crowd I feel so alone, so many people yet still so alone

Everyone else seems to be so occupied yet even in my busyness, at home, at work, at church,
Even with my family pottering around and chattering here and there,
Even with friends on the other end of the line, yet still I can feel so alone, it's as if I am not heard.

You're never alone.

Oh, Yes I am.
No you are never alone!

For God never leaves you nor forsakes you,
He's waiting patiently at your door,
He'll be there as soon as you call.

By the way did you call Him?

Section 3 leaving it behind and taking off!

Therefore if any person is (engrafted) in Christ (the Messiah) he is a new creation (a new creature altogether); the old (previous moral and spiritual condition) has passed away. Behold, the fresh and new has come.

2 Corinthians 5:17 AMP

Therefore we also, since we are surrounded by so great a cloud of witnesses, let us lay aside every weight, and the sin which so easily ensnares us, and let us run with endurance the race that is set before us.

Hebrews 12:1 NKJV

Section 3 leaving it behind and taking off!

leaving it behind and taking off!

This section of poems and inspired expressions addresses in the first instance some of the negative aspects of our lives and our pasts, then kick starts us into leaving it behind and taking off into a new dimension.

I truly believe that we have to acknowledge our past so we can learn from it, put it in perspective and then move onto what God has designed and predestined for us. As long as we walk around with the issues of our old life we are weighed down but when we address them there is a liberty that gives us wings.

Another way of expressing this is by using the example of an air balloon that can carry passengers. While the balloon is stationery it has huge sandbags as weights holding it down on the outside and some smaller weights on the inside so that it does not take off prematurely. When the passengers are safely in the air balloon the weights are released so that it can take off for its journey. To ensure that it can go to its desired heights more air is released into the actual balloon and some of the lighter weights inside the basket of the balloon must be released.

I believe this is how God works. He wants us to soar like an eagle to the heights that He has for us with the gracefulness and the lightness of the air balloon. For us to move off and achieve the heights and depths God has for us we need to cut off some of the weights that hold us in the same position. For a moment I'd like you to imagine an air balloon with your name on it. Now imagine the huge sandbags holding it down. You are scheduled to take this ride; you have been given the authority and the tools to cut off the sandbags for take off. However, first you must name the weights that have held you back and allow the Holy Spirit to work in and with you to cut them off so you can soar to the height you know is within you to achieve. For some the weights may represent fear, for others lack of faith, and for others still shame, busyness or procrastination – whatever it is, decide to cut them off so you too can soar!

Once you have taken off, God Himself will reveal to you what some of the smaller weights are that you must shed to ensure you continue your journey. For some the smaller weights may be pride, low self-esteem and/or doubt. You see, you can take off with these but they must be addressed so that you can reach higher heights.

Oh yes, and don't worry about the air that needs to be pumped into the actual balloon because the Holy Spirit is the wind that will take care of that aspect. What I appreciate about how the Lord works is that it is never just about us. Similarly, the analogy of the air balloon, the fact that it can take passengers, mirrors God's plan for us. God desires for us to be witnesses, people who can carry someone else, bring someone else along side us so they too can meet with our Saviour and King. So as you continue, also think about the lives that you can affect when you take off in the position God has set for you.

Daughter of God, it's time to make that decision to leave it behind, whatever the 'it' is in your life, and take off to a new dimension for truly your change is gonna come…

'Before I shaped you in the womb, I knew all about you. Before you saw the light of day, I had holy plans for you; a prophet to the nations – that's what I had in mind for you.'

Jeremiah 1:5 TM

wanted

An unexpected birth,
The result of an accident or tragedy;
You were not planned.
'I wanted a boy not another girl,'
The constant reminder of a love once had,
A difficult delivery,
A Cesarean,
*'I nearly died giving birth to you
In the labour ward.'*

Wanted – but was I wanted?

Last in line once again as the Captain picks his team.
Football, netball, rounders and cricket.
'Pick me, pick me, not last again,' I sigh.

Wanted!?

The party's in full flow,
Friends are singing loudly,
The pace begins to slow and it's time for the lovers dance.
'Not a wall flower, please someone notice me.'

Wanted!?

Dating the best looking partner or most popular DJ,
Wearing the latest trends: Armani, Nike, Gucci, and Kookai.

Wanted!

It doesn't work you know.

I need to prove my worth:
Trainee to Supervisor,
Supervisor to Manager,
Manager to Specialist.

It doesn't work you know.

No material or external possession puts value on your life;
No person or job gives you the love that you need.

It's the knowledge that I called you, I ordained you before your birth, while in your mother's womb,
A nurturing place for your features to be developed.

Wanted!

Yes, you're not only wanted but you're needed as well,
For my works I cannot accomplish unless through you.

Wanted!

Yes, you're wanted.
For no one else sees what I see in you.
When others saw Peter, I saw a solid rock.

Wanted!

Yes, my child,
Look for what I say about you,
The promises I give to you,
For you I sent my only child.

You see I don't only need you I want you as well.

Yes, *I am wanted.*

So don't you see that we don't owe this old do-it-yourself life one red cent? There's nothing in it for us, nothing at all. The best thing to do is give it a decent burial and get on with your new life. God's Spirit beckons. There are things to do and places to go! This resurrection life you received from God is not a timid, grave-tending life. It's adventurously expectant, greeting God with a childlike 'What's next Papa?' God's Spirit touches our spirits and confirms who we really are. And we know we are going to get what's coming to us – an unbelievable inheritance! We go through exactly what Christ goes through. If we go through the hard times with him, then we're certainly going to go through the good times with him!

Romans 8: 15-17 TM

For we are God's (own) handiwork (His workmanship), created in Christ Jesus, (born anew) that we may do those good works which God predestined (planned beforehand) for us (taking paths which He prepared ahead of time), that we should walk in them (living the good life which was prearranged and made ready for us to live).

Ephesians 2:10 AMP

who am i?

Who am I?
This question continues to be asked.
Who am I?
Every individual tries to find the answer.
Who am I?

Oh it's so hard to describe, I hear so many declare.
I'm kind,
I'm loving,
I have a good job,
I'm clever,
But the question still remains: *Who am I?*
When the going gets tough,

WHO AM I?

How many faces do I have, how many personalities,
For work, church, friends, family and strangers,
What face do I have in front of my enemies?
When I'm alone at night and in the confines of my own space?
WHO AM I?
What face do I see?

When everything appears to be going wrong,
No answers seem to come along,
Which face, which personality steps in to deal with it?
Mmh, WHO AM I?

I'll tell you *who I am* that you might affirm *who you are.*

You see, I AM WHO I AM,
I AM ME!

I am a Princess who is joint heir to the throne of grace,
So when I walk my head is held high
I deserve only the best, only excellence will do;
Only the most precious gifts are set aside for me.

Who am I?
I AM WHO I AM
I AM ME!

I have been through the rough and I have been through the smooth,
Yet all that remains is a stronger image of me.
Each battle I've faced has etched another sketch to my character,
Not one experience gone to waste,
Each one valuable in this race.

So, Who am I?
I AM WHO I AM
I AM ME!

I am strong,
I am powerful,
Vibrant, gifted,
Yes I am positive, blessed and highly favoured,
I am more than enough,
I am a beautiful aroma,
I am God's workmanship, His poetry in motion.

Who am I?
I AM WHO I AM
I AM ME!

I am a picture of health,
A picture of wealth,
I am successful,
Intelligent,
Wise and knowledgeable,

I am instinctive,
Distinctive,
Intuitive and inquisitive.

Who am I?
I AM WHO I AM
I AM ME!

I am not only a survivor but a thriver as well,
I am more than a conqueror,

When the battle raged,
And the kingdoms roared,
When my esteem was crushed,
And my self worth was torn,
When I gave away my power,
When I gave away myself,
When I gave away my dignity,
My self image and my hopes,
No one thought I'd make it,
Bar a few in my corner,
No one thought I'd achieve it,
But I was just waiting to find out
Who I am.

And now I know
That Who am I
Is WHO I AM
And that I AM ME!

I can win every battle, for My Father has gone before me;
I can write those books to inspire and transform the nations of this world;
I can speak under the anointing to bring deliverance and inspiration;
I can move by the Holy Spirit to minister healing to every emotion and every dis-ease;

Inspirations for Women . . . A Journey to Wholeness

I can stand and stand and when I've done all, I can stand,
For I stand not in my own strength but in the power of His might.

Who am I?
I AM WHO I AM
I AM ME!

A precious child of God who is wanted,
Who is needed,
Who is loved and is lovable,
Who is gentle and kind,
Who is patient and joyful,
Who has peace in abundance,
A future full of hope with success as its destiny.

Who am I?
I AM WHO I AM
I AM ME!
I am A CHILD OF GOD!
Strong, vibrant, versatile and virtuous,
Sensitive, intuitive,
A vessel of honour,
A channel of healing,
Called to restoration,
Blessed by the Father,
Led by the Spirit, saved through Christ Jesus.

Who am I?
I AM WHO I AM
I AM ME!

Pay close attention now:
I'm creating new heavens and a new earth,
All the earlier troubles, chaos, and pain
Are things of the past, to be forgotten.
Look ahead with joy.
Anticipate what I'm creating;
I'll create Jerusalem as sheer joy.

Isaiah 65: 17-18 TM

your future – a new dimension

Today's the day to make up your mind.
Today's the day to move on in the right direction;
Upwards, outwards and forwards – no backwards allowed,
For it's your future we're talking about.
A new dimension if you choose.

I feel like today is a day for decisions,
One where there'll be no looking back and no turning back,
No regrets, no *if only's* or *may be*', just some made up minds.
With one simple word you can decide
To make it or to fake it,
To go for it or reside in your comfort zone;
The choice is yours
For as you utter it, you can have it.
You see, our tongues have the power to create.

Today's the day, fellow sojourner, to go over to the progressing side.
It certainly won't always be easy,
Not everyone will like it.
Some will positively hate to see you move on
As they secretly wish it was them.
Don't let that put you off, but let it push you on!

Make a decision about your new dimension.
That's what these words are encouraging you to do.
It's preparing you, encouraging and developing you to fulfill your vision and be all God created you to be.

So make a decision that will count.
No point whispering it,
Musing on it or thinking about it.
You see, many a dream has remained in the imagination phase,
The 'one-day-I-will' phase,
'When-the-kids-get-older' phase,

'When-I-have-enough-money-in-the-bank' phase.
So many dreams rest in peace in a graveyard;
Don't let *your* dreams be one of them!

Today you choose the focus and direction for your new dimension!

You alone know what it will be.
Maybe it's that new business you've been talking about,
That expansion or specialism;
Is it that new building, that ministry, that invention you've been wrestling with?

What is it for you?
What's your future's new dimension?

You choose Sister,

And move on in it today!

If God hadn't been for us – all together now, Israel, sing out! –
If God hadn't been for us when everyone went against us,
We would have been swallowed alive by their violent anger,
Swept away by the flood of rage, drowned in the torrent;
We would have lost our lives in the wild, raging water.
Oh blessed be God!
He didn't go off and leave us.
He didn't abandon us defenseless…

Psalm 124: 1-6 TM

Section 3 leaving it behind and taking off!

woman – your change is gonna come!

If it were not for the Lord on your side, where would you be?
What would your condition in life be today?
What confusion, what trouble, what issues would have and could have consumed you, overflowed you, knocked you down, tripped you up?
If it were not for the Lord God Almighty on your side!

Today is no ordinary day,
It has been pre-ordained to be a celebration,
A celebration of your change, you're coming out,
For a change is gonna come!
No ordinary one, not one that will pass you by,
For this one has your name on it.
You reading this is no coincidence, luck or accident at all,
For today is the day for your change to come!
Right now it is being birthed in the heavenlies, manifested in the earthly places.
Some of you will have to push it out, others have to press in and press on.
In other cases a Holy Ghost operation is taking place.
For today, there is no choice, you see, if you believe it and you'll receive it,
With no doubting in your heart,

YOUR CHANGE IS GONNA COME!

I know some people thought you wouldn't make it, even thought that you were faking it,
They thought you would have given up by now,
Thought you were destined for nowhere, when in your darkest hour they cried, where is your God?
Why not curse Him and die?
They thought that marriage would have been the end of you,
That relationship would have messed you up for good,

They thought your house would have been repossessed,
You'd be walking instead of driving a new car.
They thought loneliness, misery, depression and oppression was part of your make-up – it's your lot, some have said.

But shout for joy!

Stand to your feet and declare that today, if you have to push, if you have to press, if you have to squeeze or if you have to leave some folk behind,

YOUR CHANGE IS GONNA COME!

Declare that today is the day!
It might be in this second,
It may only take a moment,
You may not feel anything,
Yet you might feel a whole lot, but whatever the emotion,
Whatever you have to do,
Look for and receive your change!

Tell your neighbours to excuse you if you shout,
Tell your friends to pardon you if you dance,
Tell your family to move out of the way as you jump,
Tell them not to worry if you cry because they don't understand where you've really been:
Where the Lord has brought you from,
And today the time is right,
The atmosphere is conducive,
I'm accepting and receiving MY CHANGE!
I'm getting ready to change my attitude as I go to a new altitude!

You see I'm tired of being weary,
Frustrated with being bruised and misused,
Fed up with not achieving all God has for me,
So today I'm declaring a national emergency in my life because my change is gonna come.
Sound the alarm, blow the trumpet because today is the day my change is gonna come.

MY CHANGE IS HERE!

I receive my change!
I receive my change!
I receive my change!
I receive my change!
I receive my change!
I receive my change!

November 7, 2000 – Written by Jacqueline Peart, Inspired by The Holy Spirit

Arise, shine;
For your light has come!
And the glory of the Lord is risen upon you.
For behold, the darkness shall cover the earth,
And deep darkness the people;
But the Lord will arise over you,
And His glory will be seen upon you.
The Gentiles shall come to your light,
And kings to the brightness of your rising.
Lift up your eyes all around, and see;
They gather together, they come to you;
Your sons shall come from afar,
And your daughters shall be nursed at your side.
Then you shall see and become radiant,
And your heart shall swell with joy;
Because the abundance of the sea shall be turned to you,
The wealth of the Gentiles shall come to you.

Isaiah 60: 1-5 NKJV

sisters arise

Sisters arise, shine for your light has come!
Sisters arise, your prayers have come up as a memorial before God this day!

Sisters from the east, from the west, north and south,
Arise for your time has come!
Whether you are from the Caribbean, India, Africa, London, Scotland, Ireland, or even a combination of them all,
Arise. The race is not the issue; culture is not what this is about,
Whether you are old or young,
Arise for your time has come!

God is about to shine His light into and onto every dark situation, every dark area in your life.
He is about to shine His light into every barren area,
Every dry area, every forgotten area,
For surely the Lord says to you today: Sisters arise.
Get up out of your comfort zones,
Get up out of your areas of familiarity and contentment,
Get up out of religiousness and traditionalism, gestures and actions.

I believe you reading this poem was not just a coincidence
But truly it is a trumpet cry from the Lord God Almighty Himself.
Truly this day has been ordained to bring us out of hiding,
Bring us out of our dark place!

Doing the dishes, dressing the children, baking cakes, or driving the right car, doing the right job and looking the part
Is not the heart of God's intention.
His intention is for us to be made whole, to be wealthy, to be purposeful.
For truly He has called us to infect, affect and effect our communities, our children and our men; truly He has called us to be role models in this end time!

So, Sisters arise!

Hear the trumpet sounding in Zion,
Hear the heart of the Father as He says to arise out of your slumber.
Some may say: 'What slumber? I've been busy working.' Another may say: 'I'm alright, it's the rest of them that need to get in line and in place!'
Whatever level, whatever place you find yourself in and on this day,
This word is for you:

ARISE!

Sister, arise!

God is coming back for a church that is spotless.
Turn to your neighbour and say: 'He's coming back for you!'
Are you ready?
Should He come tonight would you be ready?
Should He come while you're at work would you be ready?
Should He come when you're gossiping, *whoops...* I mean taking prayer requests, would you be ready?
Whatever has held you back or hindered you up until this moment,
We declare in the matchless name of Jesus Christ that it must be moved!
For I hear the trumpet of the Lord declare:

SISTERS ARISE.
HE IS CALLING YOU,
SISTERS ARISE AND BE WHOLE!

SISTERS ARISE!

You don't have to fake it,
You don't have to get up and dance like anyone else.
You see, when God is getting ready to do something new, there are so many different responses, none more holy than the other.
Though we as a church have mistaken religious and traditional shouts as anointed and holy, let's not make that mistake today,
Let's just press through and get a glimpse of His holiness, get a glimpse of His light.

You see, some of you may want to shout and holler,
Others may have to drag themselves into the holy of holies,
Some may just manage to touch the hem of His garment.
A few may be led just to weep and travail,
Others may just want to be still and know that He is Lord,
While others may jump for joy while laughing under the anointing;
Whatever you need to do, DO IT!
Don't leave until you get it!
You've prayed long enough,
You've hoped long enough, some of you have even silently given up hope!
God has a special word for you!
KEEP HOPING!

I am a God that cannot lie!
What I said I would do, I will do!
Trust Me, obey Me and watch Me work!

So, don't let anything hinder you,
Don't let anything stop you,
Let nothing cause you to miss what God is doing!

All He asks you do to is believe.
All He asks you to do is take a step of faith and ARISE!

So, Sisters arise!

And let us not grow weary while doing good, for in due season we shall reap if we do not lose heart.

Galatians 6:9 NKJV

Look to Me, and be saved,
All you ends of the earth!
For I am God, and there is no other.

Isaiah 45:22 NKJV

Come to Me all you who labour and are heavy laden, and I will give you rest.

Take My yoke upon you and learn from Me, for I am gentle and lowly in heart, and you will find rest for your souls.

For My yoke is easy and My burden is light.

Matthew 11:28-30 NKJV

Section 3 leaving it behind and taking off!

keep on going

Keep on going,
Never give in,
Keep on going,
Never give up,
No matter how the journey may seem rough,
Even though the terrains of life can feel tough,
Keep on going for this too shall pass!

My encouragement to someone today is:
That no matter what part of the journey you are on,
Whether you're at a junction or on a one way,
Keep on going,
It is worth it and so are you!

Experiences, trials and tribulations only increase our faith,
They strengthen us and mature us on this blessed walk of ours.
Some seem more intense than others,
Some trials we won't even understand, and to comfort ourselves we'll put a name to it.
Look up, don't look down,
Look up, don't look to the side,
Look up, don't look at your circumstances,
Look up, because the answer is always there,
It's always in the palm of His hands, it's always in His word.

I just want to encourage someone today
To keep on going,
Keep going on.

Your victory is already won,
Already written in the book of life,
I know we tire, some even weary as well,
But don't stop, don't lose heart,

KEEP ON GOING,
As your strength He will renew!

Section 4 celebrating my past

'At the same time,' says the Lord, 'I will be the God of all the families of Israel, and they shall be my people.'

Jeremiah 31:1 NKJV

celebrating my past

To enable us to live whole purpose filled lives, we must know where we are coming from (knowledge), learn from it (experience and reflection) and celebrate it (wisdom).

The selection of poetic expressions contained within this section acknowledges and celebrates the contribution our parents and grandparents have made in our lives, for they have a part in who we have become. Our parents and grandparents have made indelible marks on our characters. This is often borne out from others who know you well and make comments such as, 'You remind me so much of your mother/father', or 'You take such and such quality from your grandmother's side of the family'. Positive comments should be harnessed and celebrated so that we can become the best people we can be. Sometimes the comments are meant to be derogatory, but I believe that whatever is meant for evil God can and does turn it around for good.

It is always amusing how as children we say things like, 'I'll never do that when I get older' or 'I'm not going to be like my mother when I have children.' Then gradually we begin to hear some of those same sayings and ways of behaving echoed within our own lives and conversations. Decide with the help of the Holy Spirit what attributes and characters are glorifying to God and adopt and celebrate them, and for those that are no longer a reflection of who He has called you to be, make the decision to leave them behind.

I recognise that for some women reading this your experience of your mother, father and/or grandparents were not pleasant ones and for some the memories are best forgotten. May I take this opportunity to encourage you to look back at your experiences and ask God to help you locate the pearls of wisdom that you need to take from those experiences so that you do not discount every experience. There is a saying that sums this up: 'Don't throw away the baby with the bath water'. That is, don't throw away the good while you are throwing away the bad!

As I write I can almost hear someone saying, 'You don't understand. You have always had a good relationship with your family.' My response would be, *no I never*! My family is one of the most real and beautiful families I know – NOW! This has not always been the case. Since allowing God into our lives we have all embarked on our own individual journeys with God that have chipped away at and severed some of our weights and baggage. It was not an overnight process, it is an ongoing process.

So I would encourage you whatever your experience, to take the first step and let the changes start with you first. You cannot go back and change your childhood, but what you can do is choose to accept that how it was, was how it was and God was right there with you. Decide to forgive who you need to forgive, walk into your future, baggage and weight free, learning to celebrate your past so you can truly understand your present and prepare for your future.

Be encouraged as we honour our heritage…

And he will turn the heart of the fathers to the children,
And the hearts of the children to their fathers,

Malachi 4:6 NKJV

my father

My Father, my Daddy, have I told you you're my King?

My Friend who's concerned about the lives of His children,
An example for my earthly father, who is the strength in our home,
A strong deliverer is He,
He knows when to remain silent and when to speak.

My Father
Who is He?

Even as I write my heart is warmed a fresh,
Even as I think on the things that He says and has said,
I realise how faithful… and oh, how I am blessed!

My earthly father
Who is he?
A replica of my Heavenly Father

He's great,
He makes me laugh, he makes me think and on the rarest occasion he has been known to make me cry.
He always wants the best for me, my family and my friends,
The strangers and the widows.

My father
Who is he?

He is also my provider and protector!

Who is he?

He's my father,
A great Man of God!

Then He said to the disciple '…Behold your mother!'

John 19:27a NKJV

Regard (treat with honour, due obedience, and courtesy) your father and mother, that your days may be long in the land the Lord your God gives you.

Exodus 20:12 AMP

my mother

Mmh, my mother,
Patient, yet impatient,
Kind all the time,
With a bark that can equal her bite.

She's sweet, gentle, cute as well,
That's my mother folks,
Watch out, for she can hold her own.

Mmh, my mother,
Intelligent and witty,
She'll keep an audience enthralled;
Don't let her mislead you, because she's always one step ahead of the game.

Mmh, my mother,
Intuitive and honest, sometimes it hits a nerve,
Though thoughtful and generous with her love and her time
And a good money lender when you're caught short at the bank.

Mmh, my mother,
I honour you today,
Asking your forgiveness for all the days I strayed and went my own way.

To my mother, I love you.

Remember, mothers aren't perfect; they're at the University of life too!
So,

Whatever your circumstance,
Whatever your concern,
Whatever your past experience,
Whatever your hurt,
Put them behind you and honour your mother today
And tell her how much you care.
By doing so, you'll not only free yourself, but you'll free her as well.

I wrote this poem in 1998 and dedicated it to my mother a truly beautiful woman.

On the 30th December 2001 she was water baptized and for the first time gave her testimony in public as she made a real commitment to the Lord. I cannot tell you what a joy and privilege it was to see my mother (and my sister Marcia) baptised.

Why do I tell you this? Because daily she is maturing, daily she is becoming all God has declared about her in His word, her worth is far above rubies. The heart of my dad safely trusts her so he will have no lack. She does him good and not evil all the days of her life. She willingly works with her hands as she brings her food from afar. She also rises while it is yet night, and provides food for her household. She invests wisely as she girds herself with strength. She perceives that her merchandise is good and her lamp does not go out at night. She always remembers the poor, the sick and the disadvantaged.

Strength and honour are her clothing. She opens her mouth with wisdom and on her tongue is the law of kindness. She does not eat the bread of idleness and her children truly have risen up and called her blessed for she is a woman who fears the Lord!

(Proverbs 31:10-31).

Now I call her not just a beautiful woman, but a BEAUTIFUL WOMAN OF GOD who is endeavouring to be all that God has ordained her to be!

The righteous shall flourish like a palm tree
He shall grow like a cedar in Lebanon
Those who are planted in the house of the Lord
Shall flourish in the courts of our God
They shall still bear fruit in old age
They shall be fresh and flourishing
To declare the Lord is upright
He is my rock and there is no unrighteousness in Him.

[Emphasis is the author's]

Psalm 92:12-15 (NKJV)

in celebration of our elders

Cedar = Majestic, strong, built well and beautiful
Palm tree = Usefulness, endures under pressure, stand against storms, shelter – SAP DOESN'T DRY!

In celebration of our elders
A reminder that you are blessed!

Where could I possibly begin?
Where do I attempt to start?
So much richness,
Such a wealth of wisdom,
Centuries of experience,
Decades of knowledge and miles of understanding
And many a tale all wrapped up in you, my elders.
My grandaunts and uncles,
Grandmothers and grandfathers,
You all helped to raise me,
Some of you will say you don't even know me,
But as an old African saying goes,
It takes a whole village to train up a child!

It's because of your strength, your determination, your hopes and your dreams
That I have had the start that I have today!
When many of you chose and in some cases were forced to leave your home countries in hope of a better life you not only started a tradition but a legacy of hope.
You have done more in that one action than many young people today – you chose to follow the dream of a better life.
Some traveled to become doctors, carpenters, nurses and electricians, all so you could have the better life you desired!

I salute you today reminding you that you are blessed because despite the fact that many things may not have gone as you had planned it,
You followed your dream and you're still here to tell the tale!
Elders you are blessed!

Elders is such an apt and suitable name,
I recognise its biblical connotations.
Elders were always the wise of the tribes and villages
And I believe that's what you are today.
I know many would call you old age pensioners,
Others might call you old or mature people,
A few might even want to call you old *(you fill in the blank...)*
But we won't go there today!

The elders!

Today I would like to take a moment to honour you,
Take a moment to appreciate you
As well as to encourage you
That it ain't over till God says it's over!

You are blessed my beautiful elders
For you still have the sound minds God gave you.
You still know how to laugh and to have fun,
How to press on despite of and inspite of,
You do so much,
You have been through so much,
You still even desire so much!

The lines that have crept up upon your face and upon your bodies are signs of your wisdom.
Like a tree as it grows each year forming another ring,
You may develop a few more love handles, perhaps not walking as fast,
But can I tell you again, you are blessed!

Many of you have seen loved ones go,
Some of you thought you wouldn't make it after they went
But look at you now.
You are not only surviving but you are thriving as well,
But can I keep reminding you how wonderfully blessed you are!

You have memories that no one can take from you,
Every so often your eyes will light up as you remember a childhood game, an old flame or even some of those dances, like mash potato

Section 4 celebrating my past

and the likes,
You remember the good times,
And you remember the bad.
For I see in your eyes some of the tears you have cried,
Perhaps a small stream of your own you could recall.
But isn't God good as I remind you again,
Elders you are blessed!

For the bible clearly says that you are made in His own image,
That you are fearfully and wonderfully made,
That means you and I are God's masterpieces!

So again I say to you elders you are blessed!

Can I do something today,
On behalf of all the young people?

Can I ask you to forgive us?
Can I ask you to release us and let us go?

I know we say we'll call you,
I know we say we'll come round,
I know we say we'll do this and do that.
Though our intentions are honourable
This microwave society of ours has not helped us to find time for the important things like you and I!

As you read this poetic expression can you accept this as a symbol of our repentance?
As I stand in the gap for your sons and your daughters, for your nieces, nephews, brothers and sisters and even your grandchildren,
As I ask you
Please forgive us for not keeping our promises,
For not spending more time,
Believe me it is not symbolic of how we feel about you.
Just listen to us boasting about you to all our friends and neighbours, in fact to anyone who will listen.
Please release us, don't ever let bitterness take root –
I can't promise we'll do better

But I can promise you that you'll feel better
And God will honour your hearts!

When you look back and remember reading this book
Please also remember drawing a line in the sand over every broken promise or missed phone call. Decide this is a new day for you whatever your age.
Can I also take this opportunity of thanking and honouring you for who you are,
For what you've brought into society,
For the lives you've touched that you probably wouldn't even know.
Sometimes it's just a smile,
A suggestion,
A story,
A listening ear,
A shoulder to cry on,
A wise word,
An experience,
A laugh that makes us all chuckle,
A cheeky statement.
All of this has added to another's progression,
Another's learning and development.
Thank you elders for just being you!

Can I just remind you again as we celebrate you
You are blessed and you are beautiful!

Section 5 on my way to a better future

on my way to a better future

The title for this section explains itself. Once we have taken the plunge to get real and let the healing begin, we can then take a peep from behind the masks that we wear or have worn.

Once we have acknowledged the root cause of some of the masks and issues that have caused us to live less than authentic lives we are ready to leave them behind and take off!

Part of the process will mean celebrating our past so we can be ready and on our way to a better future.

Part of our journey to wholeness is acknowledging how fearfully and wonderfully God has designed us, not in a conceited way but in a way that acknowledges God's creative power at work in us. We have purpose, we have destiny, we are queens and princesses, we grow stronger each day as we recognise that we embody the virtuous woman described in Proverbs 31 and purpose is etched into our very veins.

I'm on my way to a better future, how about you?

Now we see but a poor reflection as in a mirror; then we shall see face to face. Now I know in part; then I shall know fully, even as I am fully known.

1 Corinthians 13: 12 NIV

me

When I found you Lord I got a look at me from behind a bright and clear mirror.
With your warmth and love you were able to remove the dirt and cracks.

Without you, I adapted the world's view but found it difficult to fit in.
Through you Lord, each day I find another piece of me,
Though not easy, but I find these pieces a little bit at a time.
Because of you Lord, I can stop running from an unrealistic view of me to the living well of reality I choose to run.

In you I can be strong, I can be weak and still your outstretched arms I meet.

Since I found you Lord, I've found me.

Because of you I lower my guard for I trust your every word:

Fear not, I'll never leave you nor forsake you, a broken and contrite heart I'm near.

Lord, thank you because since I've found you I have found me.

The Lord opens the eyes of the blind;
The Lord raises those who are bowed down;
The Lord loves the righteous.
The Lord watches over the strangers;
He relieves the fatherless and widow;
But the way of the wicked He turns upside down.
The Lord shall reign forever –
Your God, O Zion, to all generations.

Psalm 146:8-10 NKJV

single mothers

The mother,
The guardian all in one!
Stereotyped,
Categorised,
Pre-judged and tried as well.

It's time society woke up because
We're in technology, media, law and housing, too,
We're in development, health and social services,
Government and politics.
We're entrepreneurs,
Business women,
Today's woman,
Tomorrow's role models,
Award winners, and guess what?
We still find time for the home
Where we're spiritual teachers,
Moral developers,
Listeners,
Discipliners,
Examples.

And guess what we still find time for our friends, our families and our communities.
You see, we're the agony aunts,
The peacemakers, the trouble-shooters,
The strong-arms,
The initiators,
The prayer warriors,
The preachers and the teachers,
And guess what,
We still find time to laugh, time to cry, time to move on!

Why?

Because God has equipped us with much.
You see we know our purpose, and we know our design,
For we know who we are and why we are
So our destiny we pursue.
We know that without God in our programme
Focus is lacking, faith becomes weak and we find it difficult to go forward without feelings of inadequacy, fear and anxiety.
Then childhood and relationship pain finds room to taunt us, hinder us, sabotage our progress.

So single mothers, get with the programme!
Make sure God is on your side!
For this is a word to encourage you.

You do not have to be all things to all people,
An impossible feat to accomplish –
That's God's job to do!

You do not have to fit into a mould,
Nor allow past circumstances to put you in a cage of shame or prison of guilt.
You do not have to be Father and Mother –
That's reserved for the King of kings;
The Lord of lords is His name.

No accidents in God's kingdom,
Only preordained and predestined appointments!

You do your part and allow the Father to do His.
Read the story of Hagar, the first single mother accounted for in the Book of Life.
Read how God restores her and her child.
Isolation is not your portion,
Nor regret your middle name.

Do not let society define your power and your grace,
Only the word of God can do that.
You are a mother,
A nurturer,

A comforter,
A resting place for your offspring,
A provider – for you are a Proverbs 31 woman.

Walk tall with your head held high knowing that God is at your side;
Father and husband to you and to yours!
Single motherhood is not a sentence
For motherhood is always a gift to you, a woman.
Single because you have been 'Singled' out for this great assignment!

Walk tall, walk with confidence,
Walk in the knowledge that there are no mistakes in heaven,
Only preordained and predestined gifts of life!

So too the (Holy) Spirit comes to our aid and bears us up in our weakness; for we do not know what prayer to offer *nor* how to offer it worthily as we ought, but the Spirit Himself goes to meet our supplication and pleads in our behalf with unspeakable yearnings and groanings too deep for utterance.

Romans 8:26 AMP

For we do not wrestle against flesh and blood, but against principalities, against powers, against rulers of the darkness of this age, against spiritual hosts of wickedness in the heavenly places.

Ephesians 6:12 NKJV

stronger each day

With you Lord I grow a little stronger each day;
As a weightlifter pumps up his physical muscles
So my spiritual muscles increase.
I'm getting a little a stronger each day.

As the weeks and months go by, so you see the weightlifter's body define.
Just as my ministry develops, you see a definite call on my life.
I'm getting a little stronger each day,
Though not by sight are we able to see, but by faith we persevere.

What happens to the weightlifter when he's too old to train?
His muscles quickly disappear.

What happens to you when you're too weak to pray?
The Holy Spirit intervenes,
God's strength and wisdom is perfected.
Mmh, a little stronger each day.

My battle is not with flesh, but with the spirit realm I war.
Like a weightlifter a daily routine I must implore,
Not a day should go amiss allowing my spiritual muscles to decrease.

For with you Lord, a little stronger each day I grow.

Inspirations for Women . . . A Journey to Wholeness

A good woman is hard to find, and worth far more than diamonds.
Her husband trusts her without reserve, and never has reason to regret it.
Never spiteful, she treats him generously all her life long.
She shops around for the best yarns and cottons, and enjoys knitting and sewing.
She's like a trading ship that sails to faraway places and brings back exotic surprises.
She's up before dawn, preparing breakfast for her family and organising the day.
She looks over a field and buys it, then, with money she's put aside, plants a garden.
First thing in the morning, she dresses for work, rolls up her sleeves, eager to get started.
She senses the worth of her work, is in no hurry to call it quits for the day.
She's skilled in the crafts of home and hearth, diligent in homemaking.
She's quick to assist anyone in need, reaches out to help the poor.
She doesn't worry about her family when it snows; their winter clothes are all mended and ready to wear.
She makes her own clothing, and dresses in colourful linens and silks.
Her husband is greatly respected when he deliberates with the city fathers.
She designs gowns and sells them, brings the sweaters she knits to the dress shops.
Her clothes are well-made and elegant, and she always faces tomorrow with a smile.
When she speaks she has something worthwhile to say, and she always says it kindly.
She keeps an eye on everyone in her household, and keeps hem all busy and productive.
Her children respect and bless her; her husband joins in with words of praise.
"Many women have done wonderful things, but you've outclassed them all!"
Charm can mislead and beauty soon fades.
The woman to be admired and praised is the woman who lives in the Fear-of-God.
Give her everything she deserves!
Festoon her life with praises!

Proverbs 31:10-31 TM

who can find a virtuous woman?

Who can find a *virtuous woman*?

The Oxford dictionary defines virtue as quality, influence and moral excellence,
So in this day of modern technology, promiscuity and image consciousness,
Who can find a woman of quality, influence and moral excellence?
One who truly loves the Lord,
One who seeks for Him with her whole heart,
One who is desperate to be holy,
A woman who knows who she is, why she is,
And the direction she is going,
A woman who is whole!
One who knows her position,
Is certain about her status, regardless of what the world says,
One who is clear about her season,
When to sow and when to reap,
When to serve and when to be still,
When to buy and when to sell,
When to rest and when to work and all of this in balance,
When to speak and ssh, *when* to be *silent*!

Tell me who can find a *virtuous woman*?

We've had enough of virtual reality,
Women who appear to be one thing
Till you scratch beneath the surface.
Watch that perfect image disappear
A woman of virtue is one who is all she projects to be with no hidden surprises
We're tired of the look good but don't feel good inside
We're not looking for superwomen
Just one who relies on the supernatural power of God

Not one who is needy or one who is desperate all the time
Clinging on to anything and anyone that seems to be strong in her sight
We're looking for a virtuous woman, one of quality, influence and moral excellence
One who the bible says is blessed!

So tell me, who can find a *virtuous woman*?

Where would you begin?
When would you commence?
Who can you go to for help to find this virtuous woman?
How will you know when you have met one?
Ate with one, served one, laughed with one, ignored one quarreled with one, respected or even loved one?

Mmh, a *virtuous woman*!

One who is V for a visionary who's versatile and vibrant;
One who uses her I for integrity, innovation and intuitiveness;
One who is R for real, relevant and radical;
One who is T for tenacious and understands the language of tears;
One who is always U for understanding but never undermining;
One who is O for obedient and never overbearing;
One who is U for unique, for she is not an imitator
But who is S for special and always sensitive to what the Spirit says.
Mmh a *virtuous woman*!

You are that woman, that virtuous woman,
For in God's own image you were made,
All these gifts and qualities inside you just awaiting their release.
You are worthy to be called blessed
For you're blessed when you come and wherever you go.
You are entitled to the image for all you have been through,
The fact that you are still standing despite your setbacks, break ups and mishaps decrees that you have more on this earth to do.

You have been anointed and appointed,
You see your power is within,
For greater is He that is in you, than he that is in the world.

It's time Virtuous Woman to let your potential be released,
It's time Virtuous Woman to be all you know you can be!

For all who are led by the Spirit of God are sons of God. For (the Spirit which) you have now received (is) not a spirit of slavery to put you once more in bondage to fear, but you have received the Spirit of adoption (the Spirit producing sonship) in (the bliss of) which we cry, Abba (Father)! Father!

The Spirit Himself (thus) testifies together with our own spirit, (assuring us) that we are children of God.

And if we are (His) children, then we are (His) heirs also: heirs of God and fellow heirs with Christ (sharing His inheritance with Him); only we must share His suffering if we are to share His glory.

Romans 8: 14-17 AMP

queens and princesses

When you think of a queen and a princess what do you think of?

Royalty,
Someone who is poised and eloquent,
And full of finesse,
Someone who wears a crown and sits on a throne,
Someone who has authority and dominion.

That's what you have and that's what you are!

A queen,
A princess.

What do you think of when you think of a queen and princess?

The bible tells us that we are joint heirs with Christ Jesus,
So we hold royal status for truly we are part of a holy nation, the royal priesthood you see.

Queens and princesses,

That's who we are to Him!

It's time to stop living as paupers,
Living beneath your royal status,
You have dominion,
You have authority,
You are joint heirs to the throne of grace,
You have been adopted into the family, the marvelous family of Christ.
It's time to own it,
Walk in it!
Nothing but the best for His princess!

Who are we?

We are queens and princesses!

Section 6 from the father's heart

"This is how much God loved the world; He gave his Son, his one and only Son. And this is why; so that no one need be destroyed; by believing in him, anyone can have a whole and lasting life. God didn't go to all the trouble of sending his Son merely to point an accusing finger, telling the world how bad it was. He came to help, to put the world right again. Anyone who trusts in him is acquitted; anyone who refuses to trust him has long since been under the death sentence without knowing it. And why? Because of that person's failure to believe in the one-of-a-kind Son of God when introduced to him.

John 3: 16-18 TM

Love never gives up,
Loves cares more for others than of self.
Love doesn't want what it doesn't have.
Love doesn't strut,
Doesn't have a swelled head,
Doesn't force itself on others,
Isn't always "me first,"
Doesn't fly off the handle,
Doesn't keep score of the sins of others,
Doesn't revel when others grovel,
Takes pleasure in the flowering of truth,
Puts up with anything,
Trusts God always,
Always looks for the best,
Never looks back,
But keeps going to the end.

1 Corinthians 13: 4-7 TM

from the father's heart

The Father's heart is so caring, so tender, so sensitive, yet at the same time is so strong, so protective and authoritative. When we only perceive one facet of who God the Father is we live with a distorted view of Him. That's why some people can only see God the Father as a controller and a dominator, often because that is how they saw their own father. Others only see God as spiritual and therefore emotionally absent, again the root of this image can often be traced back to the relationship they had with their own father. Others see Him almost as a "sugar daddy" who is there to bestow gifts upon them, and when Father God does not answer as they would hope, they believe He no longer loves them or that He is punishing them for some crime.

That's not love and it's not the Father's heart.

The Father's role in His daughters' lives is that of Provider, Protector and Identity Giver.

When we connect with Father God He demonstrates these qualities, for He encompasses them all to perfection.

Think about what you believe Father God is to you. Is He just the Provider? If so you are missing His protection and lacking in your identity.

Throughout the pages of this book I pray that you saw and experienced the Father's heart for you in relation to becoming whole, which is part of His identity, putting on the mind of Christ, and being made in His image. Sisters, Father wants you to recognise who you are for your identity can only be found in Him.

Have you ever noticed how a child that has been adopted, no matter how wonderful her adopted parents are, has a deep desire to find out who her real parents are? It's natural, she wants to find out who she is.

If you want to find out who you are, go to the Father for in Him is where your identity lies and the more you find out about Him the more you find out about you.

"So I sought for a man among them who would make a wall, and stand in the gap before Me on behalf of the land, that I should not destroy it; but I found no one."

Ezekiel 22:30 NKJV

"As many as I love, I rebuke and chasten. Therefore be zealous and repent. Behold, I stand at the door and knock. If anyone hears My voice and opens the door, I will come in to him and dine with him, and he with Me.

Revelations 3:19-20 NKJV

Section 6 from the father's heart

I AM searching

As I look too and fro throughout this land,
I desired to meet with just one person who was not busy!

Busy working
Busy talking
Busy writing
Busy reading
Busy doing!

I looked for just one person who would hear My heart's cry.

One person who would share My desires,
One person who would reverence Me,
One person who would worship Me,
One person who would be with Me,
One person who would pray WITH Me!

Pray with Me you ask!

Yes pray with Me, for prayer is a two way process.
So often I hear your side,
How often do you hear My side?
How often do you wait in My presence?
How often do you tarry a while with Me, waiting for Me, desiring Me,
listening for and to Me?

So many search My word for things to back up their thinking,
back up their theology,
When I just want some more true worshippers who would return to
the Heart of true worship, return to My heart,
Some worshippers who would love Me just for Me,
Just for Me being I AM!

Deep Calleth Unto Deep

Will you be that person?
Will you be the one that makes it all about Me?

Will you be the one to go against the odds and really say and BELIEVE that it's all about Me?

Will you?
Will you seek My heart and not just My hand?

For today My child I am searching
Searching for just one!

Will you be the one?

Will you?

"Only be strong and very courageous, that you may observe to do according to all the law which Moses My servant commanded you; do not turn from it to the right hand or to the left, that you may prosper wherever you go."

Joshua 1: 7 NKJV

Then the Lord answered me and said;
"Write the vision and make it plain on tablets.
That he may run who reads it.
For the vision is yet for an appointed time;
But at the end it will speak, and it will not lie.
Though it tarries, wait for it,
Because it will surely come,
It will not tarry."

Habakkuk 2: 2-3 NKJV

"Ah, Lord God! Behold, You have made the heavens and the earth by Your great power and outstretched arm. There is nothing too hard for You.

Jeremiah 32: 17 NKJV

dare to dream!

Dare to dream *and* then to believe!

Dare means to venture or to have courage
And when I talk about dreams,
I'm not referring to day-dreaming or fantasies but the kind of dream that is inspired through and by Me, the kind of dream that becomes a reality!
The kind of dream that births visions and businesses,
The kind of dreams that changes nations and generations,
And transforms lives and minds!

So today I ask you – is anything to hard for Me who made all heaven and earth?
Then dare to dream and then to believe your dreams will come to pass!

Dare to imagine all the things you have only ever thought possible for somebody else.
Dare to do those things that until now have been reserved only for your personal thoughts and imagination.
Dare to be all you could ever be!

Dare to dream!

What's the worse that could happen if your dreams are not realised?
A broken heart
Disappointment
Fear of trying again
Embarrassment
Failure
Doubt
Uncertainty
Resentment

The list goes on and on…

Still, dare to dream *and* then to believe!

Even after I've seen the list of concerns and apprehensions you so readily prepare I still want to encourage you to dare to dream! Haven't you been through or experienced most of those things in the past nonetheless?

Did you, while dreaming and daring to walk in the fullness of life, manage to stop any of these things from happening?

No!

Wasn't your heart still broken? Didn't that child, friend or partner still walk away?
Didn't they still reject you, mock you, criticise and ostracise you?

I know they did, for they did it to My only begotten son.

So dare to dream anyway, despite the 'what ifs', 'supposings' and I've done it all 'befores'.

You see, life will happen with or without your permission!
But how it happens will depend on a decision made only by you!

So dare to dream!
I have never left you, neither will I forsaken you!
So dare to live a liberated life without pain,
Without excuses,
Without fear of this or fear of that.
Dare to dream,
Dare to worship like you've never done before,
Dare to praise Me from the depth of your heart,
Despite what you may look, feel or sound like…

Dare to dream and then to believe!

Don't wait until the kids get older.
I've taken care of them for you trained them in the way that they should go, so now they will not depart from it.
Don't wait until there's more money in your bank account

I own the cattle on a thousand hills; treasures unthinkable are stored up for you.
Don't wait until you feel able or until you've done all you know
For I have equipped you, pre-prepared before you entered the womb.
Don't wait for man's permission or until someone else has tried it.
Go with Me for you'll be a winner every time!

Just dare to dream and then to believe...

What have I been asking you to do?
What will you do today?
What have you been putting off?
What reasons have you given yourself for not achieving all your dreams?
What did they say to make you lose your confidence?
And take away your strength, tampering with your hope?

Whatever it was...I still just want to encourage you one more time...
DARE TO DREAM...
And then to believe everything you desire according to My will.
It only takes a mustard seed of faith with no doubt in your heart!

I have told you before and will tell you again,
You are worthy,
You have been called,
You have been chosen,
You are wanted,

You have been set apart and even though you might not feel like it or feel good enough, the blood of Jesus covers you, equips you and heals you.

SO...DARE TO DREAM...AND TO BELIEVE...
With Me in the centre of every hope,
Every dream and every ambition
You cannot help but win!

So will you, will you dare to dream?

"He who believes in Me, as the Scripture has said, out of his heart will flow rivers of living water."

John 7:38 NKJV

The name of was Nabal, and the name of his wife Abigail. And she was a woman of good understanding and beautiful appearance; but the man was harsh and evil in his doings. He was of the house of Caleb.

Now Abigail made haste and took two hundred loaves of bread, two skins of wine, five sheep already dressed, five seahs of roasted grain, one hundred clusters of raisins and two hundred cakes of figs, and loaded them on donkeys. And she said to her servants, "Go on before me; see, I am coming after you." But she did not tell her husband Nabal.

1 Samuel 25: 3, and 1819 NKJV

(Read 1 Samuel 25 gain a full understanding of how this woman saved her household from devastation through her wisdom and understanding... she was definitely a woman and a daughter of influence!)

rise daughter of influence

Rise daughter of influence

Not only are you a woman of influence but a woman of power.
I have surveyed your heart and brooded, yes hovered over you during this season.

Some of you have felt the changes,
Questioned the changes,
But today daughter of influence I desire to open up the dams of power within you, the dams of influence and vision.

I desire to watch you move into the place you were called.
You've wondered when,
You have questioned how long.
Daughter throughout these pages I have shown you that influence rests within you,
Power rests within you,
Wholeness resides within you!

It is time to stir up your gifts:
Like a remnant army you sit.
Choose ye this day:
Comfort zones or your will
Or do you desire the next level?

There is always discomfort with change, always uneasiness in the not knowing.

I sense some of you saying, what do I have to do, I'm not sure what is expected of me.
Don't let the enemy mislead you.
Everything I have ever done has required someone or something,
Yes, even a donkey to say yes Lord
To your will and to your way.

Are you willing to let the dams of living water flow?
Are you ready to say yes Lord, it's time for me to arise and make an impact?

It's time to arise daughter of influence!

Section 7 let the journey continue

The Lord is on my side;
I will not fear.
What can man do to me?

Psalm 118: 6 NKJV

let the journey continue

In the society that we live in now, many of us want a quick fix solution to our circumstances. We want our debts cancelled rather than to learn how to budget for and balance spending. or the latest diet pills or fad instead of living a disciplined life of healthy eating and exercise.

Unfortunately, we have brought this over to our spiritual lives. We want the quick fix. God make me better! I've prayed that prayer and even been irritated with God when I've thought about His power and majesty, how He made a donkey talk and parted the Red Sea – why then is it so difficult to answer, in my opinion, my more modest requests. God knows what will break us and what will make us. All we have to do is look at society and we can see how children when spoilt grow up to be irresponsible kids in adult bodies but those that have been given a balance of nurturing and discipline grow up to be well rounded individuals. Sadly, I seem to be seeing a lot more of the former, that is, adults that have not had balanced parenting trying to make their way in society without the love and grace of God to support them. Needless to say, the dysfunctional cycle continues.

For some of us the healing process was quick, a little like a day surgery where we go in on the same day and have a local anaesthetic. We barely see the scar and within a few days the effects of the surgery have faded away. For others it is a much longer process. Before our surgery we are prepared by the physician, informed of all the procedures that will take place, we're introduced to the anesthetist who explains all about general anaesthetic. The nurses are there to check our blood pressure, our heart rate, pulses etc., making sure we are ready for the surgery that is to take place. We take longer to come around in recovery and often there is time spent in hospital before going home to recuperate, for some the rehabilitation can take weeks for others months.

I believe it is the same process within our journey to wholeness. There is no quick fix it! We must allow the Master Physician to diagnose and determine the course of treatment for our healing. Some of us will look back and say, I don't know when it happened but God restored me, while others will have a story to tell as the deeper cut of Holy Spirit induced surgery leaves indelible marks on our memories. I believe it is important for there to be the two experiences. Those who go through more easily than others demonstrate the omnipotence of God and His miracle working power. Whereas those who take the longer route can look back and guide others through some of the processes they went through so as not to leave those going through alone or isolated when they begin their journey. Both experiences have lessons to be learnt.

Where are you?

Remember wholeness is a journey. Just like the author of the *Pilgrims Progress* we meet different people, characters and situations along our journey. Every character is important to enabling us to arrive at the place we need to be and that's in Christ, undeniably, engrafted, in tune and in step with His plans and His purpose for us.

So today, wherever you find yourself in your journey to wholeness turn your focus upwards because as much as books like these can support you and encourage you, ultimately, it will be the Father Himself that directs your path on your journey.

So Sisters, let the journey continue…

You're blessed when you're at the end of your rope. With less of you there is more of God and his rule.

You're blessed when you feel you've lost what is most dear to you. Only then can you be embraced by the One most dear to you.

You're blessed when you're content with just who you are – no more, no less. That's the moment you find yourselves proud wonders of everything that can't be bought.

You're blessed when you've worked up a good appetite for God. He's food and drink is the best meal you'll ever eat.

You're blessed when you care. At the moment of being 'care-full', you find yourselves cared for.

You're blessed when you get your inside world – your mind and heart – put right. Then you can see God in the outside world.

You're blessed when you show people how to cooperate instead of compete or fight. That's when you discover who you really are, and your place in God's family.

You're blessed when your commitment to God provokes persecution. The persecution drives you even deeper into God's kingdom.

Matthew 5: 3-10 TM

wholeness equals more of God!

More of God = wholeness
Wholeness = more of God!

As I journey along life's highway
I recognise more than ever
That I am in need of a compass (Word of God),
A companion (Holy Spirit), and
Direction (Christ Jesus).
More than ever, I recognise
I am in need of God!

On your journey to wholeness remember that the more you have of God is the more you find you!

For truly wholeness equals more of God and less of you!

Section 7 let the journey continue

woman of influence

A woman of influence is:

I	for	Influential
N	for	Necessary
F	for	Favoured of the Lord
L	for	Loved and Lovable
U	for	Unique
E	for	Exactly what God called me to be
N	for	Noble, that means you possess excellent qualities
C	for	Courageous, for if you knew what I'd been through
E	for	Eager to learn, elegant in stature, effective in calling, enduring in hard times, excellent in all things, eligible for the title of woman

W	for	Wise
O	for	Obedient
M	for	Mother, multiplier and yes money-lender!
A	for	Ambassador and
N	for	Nurturer

Deep Calleth Unto Deep

Section 7 let the journey continue

prayer of commitment

The only really effective thing you can do next is to pray, and as you pray this prayer with me believe what you are saying, invite the Holy Spirit to join you, and feel His comfort around you.

Dear Lord Jesus Christ

Thank you for life, for breath and for all you do, even when I am not aware of it you are covering and protecting me,
Thank you.
Lord I admit that I have sinned and gone my own way,
I am sorry!
I confess the times when I knowingly and unknowingly hid my true self to be accepted by man,
I need your forgiveness.
I am willing to turn away from all that I know is wrong, that includes the things that I have convinced myself is right, because I want to go with you.
I want you to be first in my life.
Thank you for dying on the cross to take away my sins.
Thank you for your gift of forgiveness, wholeness and a new life.
I now take your gift.
I ask you to come into my life by your Holy Spirit.
Come in to fill my life.
Come in as my Saviour, Counsellor and Lord forever.
I thank you Lord Jesus.
Amen

If you have taken this step of faith for the first time, find yourself a church where you can meet other Christians and find out more about Jesus Christ.

Then purchase a bible so that you can discover what God wants to say to you.

About the author
Jacqueline Peart

Inspirational Speaker ♦ Poet ♦ Author ♦ Trainer

Jacqueline is the youngest of three sisters born in east London. Like many others her life moved along often searching for more, but never sure what that 'more' was. Jacqueline found what she was looking for in January 1995 when she found Jesus Christ and became a Christian. Since then her life has turned around in more ways than one.

It's hard to believe that Jacqueline did not like or write poetry before she began writing her first book in the Deep Calleth Unto Deep Series, in May 1997.

Her ministry is unique! She shares a message of healing, hope, and restoration as she encourages and challenges us to live purpose filled lives. As a person Jacqueline is very 'real', open, honest and transparent. It is through this and her messages that many have opened the door to allow the Holy Spirit to work miraculously in their lives.

Jacqueline also runs her own training and development company, Training With Purpose, offering high quality training and development solutions to church and secular organisations alike. In addition to this busy schedule, she speaks at and organises conferences and workshops using her poems, experiences and books to take us on a journey.

As you peel back the pages of her books you will find warmth that is ever present as in Jacqueline herself. With all that's negative in life Jacqueline offers you something that's positive!

Section 7 let the journey continue

STAY IN TOUCH!

If this or any of the publications by Jacqueline Peart have blessed you and you want to let her know please write to the address below:

United Kingdom:

>   PO Box 23606
>   London, England
>   E7 9TS

United States:

>   PO Box 220
>   Uniondale
>   New York
>   11553

Email:

Info@deepcallethuntodeep.com

Website:

www.deepcallethuntodeep.com or www.deeppublishing.com

Other books in the Deep Calleth Unto Deep Series by the author:

In Search of Wholeness
Relationships
Images
Singleness